BEDTIME
Story Time

Written By Paul Doherty
Illustrated by Asia C. Shanahan Jewett

To order additional copies of this book, contact:
Xlibris LLC
1-888-795-4274
www.Xlibris.com
Orders@Xlibris.com

Dedication

To my daughters, whose love of my bedtime stories gave me the incentive to imagine, and create new and better stories each night. I will cherish those memories forever.

He ran his fingers through their hair, and said its time for bed. They looked at him with tired eyes, and shook their little heads.

Awe! Come on dad, it's not that late, they pleaded and they whined. He said "Let's go", now move your butts, its bed time story time.

They giggled when they heard the news. They loved his stories so. He made them up inside his head, and told them soft and slow.

A magic kingdom. A princess fair.
He'd gaze into their eyes, and spin
a tale right from his heart, that
sometimes made him cry.

They never knew the ending. A different one each night.

No matter how he told it, it always seemed just right.

He gave them lots of kisses.
Between the lines he read.

Your favorite place in all the world, is in your cozy bed.

So close your eyes my darlings, and let your dreams begin.

I've filled them with the purest love,
a Father could put in.

Printed in the United States
By Bookmasters